HAUNTED
LONG ISLAND

LYNDA LEE MACKEN

HAUNTED LONG ISLAND

ISBN 0-9755244-0-2

Cover design:
Debra Tremper
Six Penny Graphics, Fredericksburg, VA

Back cover logo design:
Glenda Moore, catStuff Graphics

Printed on recycled paper by
Sheridan Books, Ann Arbor, MI

CONTENTS

INTRODUCTION

Over a decade ago, Lee Moorhead, "Psychic of the Hamptons," visited a "Gold Coast" mansion on Long Island's North Shore. During dinner she noticed an older woman dressed in a black coat and hat and holding a large bag, standing in the doorway. Thinking she was the housekeeper, the psychic interrupted the conversation to tell her hostess that the woman wanted to speak with her.

"What woman? There's no one else in the house."

No *living* soul, that is.

This is just one of the many lingering spirits that populate Long Island.

Haunted Long Island explores New York State's Nassau and Suffolk Counties' supernatural history, blending ancient spirits with modern day specters to chronicle Long Island's intriguing tales and legends.

Lighthouses, mansions, restaurants and resorts, historic homes, and even a haunted windmill, tingle with otherworldly energies that startle the unsuspecting and mystify the living.

The Island's eerie history dates to its Native American inhabitants; chilling tribal legends flourish while restless natives seek peace at Montauk Manor.

Dutch colonials lived and died here – some left their essence behind and still frequent their ancient dwellings as in Centerport's Suydam House. Extraordinary tales of early settlers, such as Annie Greenleaf, can cause a shiver or two.

Revolutionary specters create spooky stirrings at historic Raynham Hall, Execution Rocks, the Country House Restaurant, and Sagtikos Manor, and their spirits wander along storied Sweet Hollow Road.

A few affluent spirits still linger at their spectacular North Shore haunts and, sadly, wraithlike children seek earthly playmates, stuck as they are in the mortal realm.

But what causes these hauntings? Although ghosts have existed for eons, no one knows for sure but most agree on a few basic explanations for earthbound entities.

Some spirits stay attached to a particular place because they are confused and don't realize they're dead. Perhaps they met with a sudden or traumatic end and are in a state of shock, stuck in the secular realm.

Intense emotions could produce a "residual" haunting, where an event is so embedded in the environment, it plays over and over, trapped in time similar to an endless audiotape or videotape, like the eerie organ melodies that manifest at dime store magnet F. W. Woolworth's "Winfield" or the image of the spectral female seen floating in the marble palace's garden. The person's corporeal life force may not actually be present; only its impression remains.

Some hang around to take care of unfinished business, like righting a wrong. This could be the case at the former Normandie Inn, or Reid's Ice Cream Factory.

Uncover the eccentric personalities who've provoked mysterious post-mortem phenomena, and the untimely deaths, disappearances, and unsolved murders that have produced an enduring and haunting heritage on Long Island.

SAGTIKOS MANOR
Bay Shore

The Sagtikos Manor property was originally owned by Dutchman Stephan Van Cortland one of Long Island's first five patentees.

In the late 17th century Van Cortland purchased a "neck" of land from the Secatogue Indians. The 150 acres formed a shape that resembled a hissing snake, hence the Indian name "Sagtikos;" the Dutch called it Apple Tree Neck.

The original section of the Manor house went up around 1692. Additional construction added rooms to the house in the 18th century, including the space where George Washington slept during his tour of Long Island in 1790.

Robert David Lion Gardiner inherited the estate in 1935 and, recognizing the property for its historic value, held open houses for the public.

In 1964 the Sagtikos Historic Society came into being to help interpret and provide tours of the site. Sagtikos Manor was listed on the National Register of Historic Places in 1976.

Stories abound that a young Revolution-era girl haunts the house and its environs. The unknown specter may be Long Island's legendary "Lady in White" because apparently her sightings have caused numerous car accidents near the property.

Stories abound that a young Revolution-era girl haunts Sagtikos Manor and its environs.

The Long Island Paranormal Hunters Association conducted investigations at the historic site. They captured orbs of light and ectoplasm with their digital cameras.

Usually orbs appear in areas where spirits are present. To theorize, these transparent, circular balls of light are the manifestation of energy being transferred from a power source, such as electric cables, heat energy in the atmosphere, batteries, or people, to the spirit(s) so they can take form. The entity may not even be aware of this process, but is just acquiring energy in a natural way. In accordance with Physics, transferring energy assumes the shape of a sphere.

Ectoplasm is a spiritual residue. This phenomenon became famous during the Spiritualist movement in the late 19th century. Ectoplasm can take many forms, but in photographs often shows up as a smoky haze when a ghost gets in the way of a shot.

Sometimes the foggy residue can be spotted floating in the air; its appearance will sometimes be an indication that a full-bodied apparition is in the process of materializing.

REID'S ICE CREAM WAREHOUSE
Blue Point

For over 80 years Reid's Ice Cream warehouse blotted the South Shore landscape. Abandoned and left to ruin, the building finally came down in 2003.

According to Sue Smitten in *Ghost Stories of New York State*, prior to its demolition the insistent shaking of its heavy metal doors baffled crewmen. Was the building protesting its demise or were its earthbound occupants?

In the 1950s a female dancer from the popular Shoreham nightspot was brutally raped and murdered. Her body was dumped on Reid's property; her killer never found.

Locals were aghast when the apparition of a young woman floated across the property and faded before their eyes. Many felt the victim's spirit haunted the spot because her terrible death went unpunished. Spectral screams and cries for help were other chilling reminders.

A young boy's spirit lingered inside the deserted depot. He fell to his death while playing there in the 1970s. Passersby reported sounds of giggling and singing coming from inside the building.

NORMANDIE INN
Bohemia

"**M**aria" is the enduring ghost at Bohemia's former Normandie Inn restaurant. During the building's days as a speakeasy, a savage strangling left a woman dead in the back upstairs bedroom.

Soon after her demise, the woman's spirit started wandering the inn. While serving as a guesthouse, visitors reported her ghost sashaying down the hallway. During the night, the restless spirit would knock on doors. When the occupants answered, they were greeted with an ice-cold breeze and nothing more.

Maria's shadowy figure knows its way around the kitchen. Inexplicable cold spots, indecipherable whispers, and unidentifiable noises hold sway along with sightings of her furtive shade moving about the cook space, the epicenter of the restaurant's paranormal activity.

Maria's most common manifestation showed up as footprints in the carpeting. For reasons unknown, this anomaly only occurred during winter months. Once, when new carpets were installed, a strange event happened. The foam padding, laid down the day before, showed mysterious footprints when the doors were opened the next day.

Today the building showcases an interior design firm and offers Maria a chic new space to make her mark.

HERMITAGE OF THE RED OWL
Brentwood

Over 150 years ago, two social reformers created a utopian community on the sparsely settled woods of Islip Town – land that is now part of Brentwood. Josiah Warren and Stephen Pearl Andrews' ultimate goal for their members was to live life in perfect harmony and with absolute freedom.

For 13 turbulent years, "free love" was the norm; couples cohabited with or without marriage and consequently brought about the Modern Times community's nickname: "Sodom of the Pine Barrens."

The village operated peacefully and was crime free so there was no need for police – all residents were afforded total freedom as long as their actions hurt no one else. Profit making was unknown; all necessities – food, clothing, land and housing, were sold at cost.

Modern Times was the last of about fifty experimental American communities in the mid-19th century. In 1945, Helen Beal Woodward wrote in a magazine article that, "Those towns stood for everything eccentric – for abolition, short skirts, whole-wheat bread, hypnotism, phonetic spelling, phrenology, free love and the common ownership of property."[i]

While walking the woods one frigid winter's day in 1877, Modern Times member Charles Godman came upon a red owl nearly frozen to death. He carefully transported the creature to his cabin and began to nurse the bird back to health.   After a while, Godman claimed the owl began to speak to him.

The red owl alleged that he was the spirit of an Indian chief named Oriwos. The owl told the Good Samaritan that a warring tribe murdered him and that his spirit would wander the earth until his skeletal remains were found and buried. As soon as the owl finished his story he vanished from sight.

Godman felt obligated to free the bird from its plight. He set off in search of Oriwos' bones, which he soon discovered in a ravine behind his cabin under a pine tree.

Three days after Godman buried Oriwos' bones where he found them, the red owl reappeared to Godman and thanked him.

Godman, moved by his experience, painted a portrait of the owl, wrote a book about his experience and named his cottage the "Hermitage of the Red Owl."

Protective spirits inhabit the historic Suydam House.

SUYDAM HOUSE
Centerport

John C. Suydam descended from Dutch ancestors who settled in Flatbush in 1678. He and his wife Abigail built their Centerport farmhouse sometime between 1710 and 1730. They planted orchards, cultivated vegetables, tended grape arbors, and erected outbuildings in support of their land. In addition to farming, the family made their living by carpentry, oystering, and shipbuilding.

The outbuildings no longer exist and the original occupants have long passed but there are those who feel some members of the Suydam family are still in residence.

The Greenlawn-Centerport Historical Association maintains the historic home at Route 25A and Spring Road that typifies an 18th century Dutch farmhouse. One of the structure's exceptional features is the large central chimney into which three fireplaces connect.

In 1990, the historical society built a replica of the barn that once stood on the property. A portion of the weathered barn museum depicts an authentic blacksmith and carpentry shop.

As stated in *Huntington's Hidden Past,* a caretaker who lived in the ancient house said she often felt a presence brush by her even when there were no windows or doors open to create a draft. The custodian felt the spirits protected the property and she would greet her unseen roommates with a hearty "Good morning!" each day.

The Inn on the Harbor was once a bawdy whaler's hangout and traces of past events used to linger in the ancient structure.

VAN AUSDALL HOTEL
(Currently The Inn on the Harbor)
Cold Spring Harbor

The old whaling town of Cold Spring Harbor bears an intriguing history that dates to a 19th century waterside tavern – the present day Inn on the Harbor. With a structure this old, ghostly tales proliferate...

Whalers favored the harbor town. The port offered rest and refreshment for the tired seamen at the Van Ausdall Hotel. The inn served as a brothel as well. Lonely townswomen often worked the bar to quell their craving for the warmth and comfort of human companionship.

In *Huntington's Hidden Past,* the author tells that a whaler found his wife upstairs with another man. In a blind rage the whaler murdered his woman and her seafaring companion, a Mr. Van Whether.

Psychics assert that Van Whether's spirit is still adrift in the ancient edifice.

A previous owner shared the tale of a woman who expired in the restaurant's ladies room. The patron met her untimely death by way of a freak accident. Intuitives claim her spiritual presence remains behind.

A third entity at the old inn frightened off a clairvoyant who attempted to cleanse the place of its psychic debris.

When former proprietors refurbished the building they discovered an underground tunnel used to smuggle liquor into the tavern during prohibition. Old bottles were strewn about the secret burrow.

Strange goings-on transpired during the renovations in 1982. Lights turned on and off for no reason, music played without cause, doors opened and slammed shut of their own volition.

In the rooms on the third floor, where the brothel once flourished well over a hundred years ago, boxes flew through the air. The murky atmosphere caused workers difficulty breathing. Eventually staffers refused to enter the storage room.

The third floor no longer exists; cathedral ceilings now grace the interior of the elegant restaurant.

It seems like the spirits have left too, if they ever existed at all...when it comes to ghosts you can never be really sure.

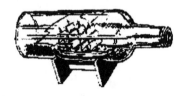

WICKHAM FARMHOUSE
Cutchogue

The Cutchogue Green Historic Buildings complex includes the Wickham House, one of the North Fork's oldest, as well as one of New York State's rarest English-style houses.

Built in 1740, the farmhouse shelters a gruesome tale.

On June 2, 1854, an insane Irish farmhand wielded an axe and murdered James and Francis Wickham in their bedroom along with a servant boy.

An extensive manhunt produced Nicholas Behan who was hanged in Riverhead for the crimes.

In 1988 family descendants awoke to witness a male apparition standing at the foot of their bed brandishing an axe. Immediately the couple sealed off the room and relocated to another bedroom.

The bloody story endures, told year after year during autumn hayrides, and although the master bedroom is still off limits, the sound of the murderer brazenly stomping down the hall toward the haunted chamber still echoes. [ii]

LLOYD'S ANTIQUES
Eastport

Lloyd Antiques holds more than ancient artifacts and curios. On the word of proprietor Lloyd Gerard, the place houses the spirit of Gerard's great-great-great-great-uncle, Andrew Simon Levi.

In 1998, Gerard shared some interesting family history with *Newsday* staff writer Jerry Zezima along with a bit of mystery that surrounds the strange events that transpire in the shop.

Andrew Simon Levi emigrated from Russia in 1860 and made a living on Long Island peddling goods to farmers and their families. Levi wore a backpack and lugged two suitcases full of household necessities such as pots and pans and needles and pins "from Brooklyn to Montauk to Greenport to Orient." Levi's sales route took two months to complete and when he finished his circuit, he trudged back to New York City to replenish his stock and begin his route all over again.

Gerard's grandfather, Harry Goldstein, once owned the building that houses Lloyd's Antiques and he peddled with Uncle Levi until he married and settled in Eastport. It appears that Uncle Levi, however, continues his sales pitch from the other side.

Once a customer came back to the store to purchase a $65 table he had seen on the second floor the week before. Gerard was puzzled – the table was priced at $400. When the buyer related the encounter with a bearded old man,

Gerard realized the patron's description matched Uncle Levi. Gerard ended up selling the table for $65.

150 years ago, Uncle Levi walked for miles to make a sale, but these days Uncle Levi's territory seems to be the second story of the antique shop. Several people have seen the man's specter peering out over the town from the large second floor window.

According to Gerard, his easygoing uncle liked to play practical jokes. When books fly off their shelves or other merchandise moves around, Gerard blames his long ago relation and feels that Uncle Levi is merely carrying on his business from beyond the grave.

Fire Island Lighthouse
(U.S. Coast Guard Photo)

FIRE ISLAND LIGHTHOUSE
Fire Island

Located on a barrier island along the south shore of Long Island between the waters of the Great South Bay and the Atlantic Ocean, Fire Island Lighthouse sits at the eastern most side of Robert Moses State Park on Fire Island.

The black-banded beacon served as an important landmark for transatlantic ships coming into New York Harbor at the turn of the last century. For many European immigrants, the Fire Island Light was their first sight of land upon arrival in America.

Long before Fire Island became a popular summertime destination, the mysterious island was a desolate place where pirates, wreckers, and the ghosts of their victims wandered.

The first Fire Island Lighthouse pierced the sky in 1825; the foundation just a few steps from the present striped lighthouse completed in 1858.

Local lore says that the caretaker of the 1825 light hanged himself and the old keeper's spirit moved in to haunt the present station.

Supernatural accounts of heavy doors slamming baffle; no wind is strong enough to blow the heavy portals open. Who, or what, can explain this mystery?

Another oddity – at times the topmost windows rise on their own; normally a long pole has to be used to open them.

Visitors report sounds of unusual laughter and someone knocking when no living soul occupies the light. Unaccountable cold spots persist throughout, a common signal of a ghostly presence.

Although not directly attributable to the haunting activity here, another eerie occurrence is that, on occasion, human skulls and various other skeletal parts washed up on the beach directly in front of the lighthouse.

The bones might be the mortal remains of prisoners and slaves once confined to ships moored off the Long Island coast during the 18th century.

MORGAN HALL
Glen Cove

Between 1900 and the end of World War I, the Island's rural North Shore community of farmers and fishermen became an exclusive enclave known as the "Gold Coast." During this time, some of the nation's most affluent citizens erected grand estates here – among them, financier John Pierpont Morgan.

By the time he was 38 years old, J. P. Morgan & Co. had grown into one of the most powerful banking houses in the world and became the world's first billion-dollar corporation. One of the firm's numerous achievements included the formation of the United States Steel Corporation.

As a yachtsman, Morgan's *Columbia* captured the America's Cup twice. A notable collector of books, paintings, and, other art objects, Morgan sponsored the American Museum of Natural History, the Metropolitan Museum of Art (of which he was president), Harvard University (particularly its medical school), and several New York trade schools.

True to form, the financier's spirit took up permanent residence inside his 1910 Nassau County estate.

Initially the Russian Embassy held title to the property, and then the Catholic Church used the mansion as a nunnery and school. The presence of the young girls seemed to trigger a series of odd occurrences in 1965.

Without the aid of human hand, windows slowly slid open and then would promptly bang shut. The filmy figure of old man Morgan floated through the students' rooms leaving an icy chill in its wake. Loud disembodied footsteps echoed in the cavernous halls.

Originally the novitiates attributed all the paranormal activity to Morgan, but changed their minds when they witnessed the spirit of a girl dressed in a long black gown. They deduced the spirit was Alice, J. P.'s daughter, who succumbed to typhoid fever at an early age.

John Pierpont Morgan supposedly haunted his magnificent mansion that was demolished in 1985.

WINFIELD HALL
Glen Cove

More than any other region in our nation, Long Island's Gold Coast glittered with private mansions, exclusive country clubs, polo fields, and marinas. Estate owners sought to outdo each other in grand displays of opulence.

In 1917, five and dime store magnate, Frank Winfield Woolworth erected "Winfield," a magnificent sixty-two-room mansion that boasted, among other appointments, solid gold bathroom fixtures and a 1,500 square foot, fourteen-carat gold gilded dining room ceiling.

Other architectural elements included secret tunnels and hidden chambers, features that shed light on the personality of its unconventional builder.

The visionary retailer was born in Rodman, a small town in upstate New York. The son of a farmer, Woolworth rejected rural life; he aspired to be a merchant.

He opened his first store in 1879 and sold discounted merchandise at the fixed price of five or ten cents, which undercut local merchants. This type of trade was in contrast to the then common practice of haggling.

Woolworth's store placed products out for the shopping public to handle, select, and purchase as opposed to earlier shops where merchandise was kept behind the counter and customers presented the clerk with a list of items they wished to purchase.

Some say F. W. Woolworth and his family members have never left "Winfield," the dime store magnet's opulent mansion.

The five and ten cent stores integrated lunch counters that served as everyday gathering places, a precursor to the modern shopping mall food court.

Many stores later, a corporate headquarters, the 60-story Woolworth Building in Manhattan, went up in 1913. The construction cost $13.5 million, which Woolworth paid for in cash.

Back then, the center of operations was the tallest building in the world and it remains one of the oldest, and one of the most famous, skyscrapers in New York City. After more than ninety years, the Woolworth Building is still one of the fifty tallest structures in the United States.

Two years after he built his ornate North Shore manor Woolworth succumbed to an acute infection caused by his decaying teeth, (he was petrified to go to the dentist).

The estate was then owned by the Reynolds family of Reynolds Aluminum Foil fame, housed a charm school, and finally went up for auction.

While attending the public sale, Oyster Bay resident Monica Randall met an enigmatic businessman who bought the onerous estate. After a whirlwind romance, Randall became engaged to Winfield's new owner, and moved into Woolworth's dream house.

Randall authored *The Mansions of Long Island's Gold Coast*, and wrote a chilling and fascinating, non-fiction account of her nightmarish experiences while living in the mysterious manse; *Winfield* (2003) chronicles the tycoon's eccentricities and the paranormal happenings at the ominous dwelling.

A renowned psychic claimed the house was full of negative spirits, subtle energies that drained and tormented its living residents.[iii] Randall, who resembled a woman who had scorned Woolworth in life, raised the wrath of Woolworth's wraith by residing in the woman's room.

In essence, Woolworth's spirit stayed behind because he refused to accept his death. The same force of character that enabled his success kept him earthbound.

The misty apparitions of F. W. and his daughter, Edna, who committed suicide, appeared during a séance held in the mansion. It is widely reported that the night Edna died, a bolt of lightning struck the coat of arms, which featured etchings of all the family members, and cracked through the impression of Edna's face.

Just about anyone who ever worked at Winfield, and some of the charm school students, witnessed a female apparition strolling through the garden and in some of the upstairs rooms.

The Italian Renaissance manse provided the perfect backdrop for the supernatural strains of spectral organ music that echoed in the spacious structure on occasion.

The mansion is built entirely of marble, which contains quartz crystals, silica, and ferric salts. These substances are used in making recording equipment, so scientists speculate that marble can trap vibrational sounds and store them for an indefinite period.[iv] This theory could account for the organ music and indiscernible mumblings Randall, and others, heard in the haunted house.

ANNIE GREENLEAF
Huntington

To this very day, they say the ghost of Annie Greenleaf wanders the woods were she once lived.

In the 17th century Annie lived alone in a tiny hut and survived as an herbalist by treating those who were sick with her natural remedies. Some townsfolk considered her a witch.

Over time, Annie grew old and bent and needed help. She became too feeble to fetch her own firewood or perform other heavy chores so she enlisted the aid of a man named Tom.

To show her appreciation, Annie promised to help the young man in any way she could.

Tom ultimately declared that he had fallen in love with a woman in town and in order to win her affection, he wanted to capture the beautiful white deer he had seen in the forest. Strangely, the animal kept eluding him however. Living so close with nature, was there any way Annie could help?

"Anything but that," begged Annie, but the man insisted – he needed Annie's assistance. Being a woman of her word, Annie told Tom he could catch the deer by shooting it with a silver bullet.

Back at his house, the expectant suitor detached the silver buttons from his father's coat, melted them down, and poured the molten liquid into bullet molds. He then set off into the woods, armed with his magic bullets, in hot pursuit of the mystifying white deer.

He tracked the animal for hours and at last, there she stood in majestic splendor. Tom took careful aim and shot the beauty through her proud white breast. The injured animal took off through the woods toward Annie's hut with Tom following closely behind.

When he finally arrived at Annie's hut there was no deer, only the old woman on her bed – dead from a bullet wound in her chest.

BRUSH-MUNGER FARMSTEAD
Greenlawn

Huntington's Hidden Past maintains that a ghost – or two, inhabits the Brush-Munger house on Greenlawn Road, named after the early families who lived in the house.

The author states that shortly after the new owners moved into the Victorian manse, and refurbished their new home, strange events took place.

The pair owned several pets and the wife distinctly heard someone with a comforting voice talking to their cats and dogs downstairs. Who could it be? Her husband was out back in the yard.

The new owners definitely felt a "presence" inside the house. The carpenter felt it too. They all could "feel" an invisible someone entering the rooms during the day. Oddly, doors opened and closed as if the unseen occupant was walking through the doorways.

Other unexplainable phenomena included the sound of furniture moving across the floor, the scent of perfume, and disembodied sighing.

The spectral tenant's most dramatic manifestation was his appearance at the window as the couple arrived home one night. Thinking the man a burglar, they cautiously inspected the residence but found no one – nor was anything disturbed or missing.

Previous owners remained tight-lipped about any eerie occurrences but the twinkle in their eyes belied the house's haunted past.

MELODY EQUESTRIAN CENTER
Huntington

Melody Equestrian Center is a hidden jewel set in the picturesque West Hills section of Huntington. Originally a farm established in the 1700s, some of the earliest buildings remain, first and foremost, the 2½ storied, gabled farmhouse.

The present owner, Joan Boesch, who boarded her horse at the stables, had her dreams realized when the property went on the market.

Since she and her husband lived only two blocks away, they planned to use the old farmhouse for the help, but Joan felt "drawn" to the cozy residence and upon entering, immediately felt at home. Eventually, the couple moved into the centuries old dwelling and restored the 22-room house to its original floor plan.

Joan's daughter was the first to stay overnight and even when all the windows were closed, often discerned a persistent breeze brush past her during the night.

Frequently, the third floor lights seemed to have a spontaneous will. Once, Joan turned them off after cleaning the upstairs and as she drove away from the house that night, she noticed they were on. When she arrived back home, the third floor was dark.

A previous owner experienced the same anomaly and alleged that a phantom played the piano during the night. When he went to visit his old place all the doorbells started ringing as soon as he set foot in the door.[v]

SWEET HALLOW ROAD & MARY'S GRAVE
Huntington

The spooky tales of Sweet Hallow Road and Mary's Grave merge with each other so often, where one legend ends and the other begins is hard to discern...

Long Island's most notorious haunted byway is Sweet Hallow Road. The road is steeped in ghostly legend – dark woods border the narrow, twisting road and a wayside cemetery lends mystery to the folklore.

The proverbial "lady in white" figures prominently in the stories. Supposedly a hefty number of drivers have witnessed her diaphanous apparition. The predominant tale claims she's the spirit of a witch hung on Long Island in the 1600s. They say she boldly walks into oncoming traffic, terrorizing drivers, and then vanishes.

Another version is that the apparition is the ghost of a young girl struck down by a car in the 1920s. Her spirit strolls the Sweet Hallow Road in the dead of the night.

One account says a newly wed couple died in an auto accident on the road. The phantom groom still looks for his bride along the road and he walks out in front of the cars that flash their headlights at him.

And then there's the story about a girl hitching a ride to get home from the prom who vanishes before the drive is over.

Individuals reported glimpsing revenants of Native Americans as well as Revolutionary War wraiths prancing in the dense woods.

Yet another tale tells of burning embers that mysteriously appear in the road, perhaps presaging danger. The glowing coals don't help the phantom driver whose car careens down the road at breakneck speed and lurches off the road. When witnesses rush into the marsh to help out the errant motorist, they are befuddled when nothing is found.

One driver reported a grim column of spectral children marching along the road.

The unusual stories about Sweet Hallow Road continue on and on and possess as many twists and turns as the mythical road itself.

There are as many "Mary's Graves" on Long Island as there are scenarios about Sweet Hallow Road. The towns of Huntington, Patchogue, Port Jefferson, Sayville, St. James, and Smithtown carry on Mary's story as well. Mary's grave in Huntington is in the cemetery on Sweet Hollow Road, (of course).

One legend says Mary nursed sick children, but when several in her care died of the pox she suffered the accusation of witchcraft and was stoned to death. Mary hovers near the place of her death, tenderly stroking the hair of children who happen to walk by according to folklorist Lisa Galloway.

Another variation says her witchcraft trial resulted in a trip to the gallows in the 17th century. In keeping with historians, this popular theory is unlikely because the only known Long Island witch-hunts occurred in East Hampton, Setauket, and Southampton.

Another story says her jealous boyfriend believed she cheated on him and while driving down the infamous Sweet Hollow Road he pushed her out of the car. Her injured body lay in the street until it was struck dead by a passing car. Her restless wraith walks the road for eternity looking to find her killer and avenge her death.

Then there's the one that involves Mount Misery, a hill named by locals who said it was such a misery getting over the hill with a horse and buggy. In 1851, a house on the hill burned to the ground although no historical records exist to substantiate the claim. Mary supposedly perished in the blaze and haunts Mount Misery. Burning embers materialize (as they do on Sweet Hallow Road) and the dead girl's blood-chilling screams fill the air.

Some allege that the ingénue was assaulted, and then murdered by two young thugs. Her killers were tried and found guilty, but before sentence could be passed they showed up dead in their jail cells. Thereafter, each year on the anniversary of her death Mary leaves her grave to exact revenge on two more men.

No matter what the particulars, Mary's life ended tragically and therefore her soul cannot rest.

For generations Mary's story has been passed down, the same story never told twice – but that's the stuff of folklore and Mary's story endures as an integral piece of Long Island's haunted heritage.

LADY OF THE LAKE
Lake Ronkonkoma

Formed by ancient glaciers, Lake Ronkonkoma is the largest of Long Island's freshwater lakes. Mostly the lake is less than 15 feet deep, but portions of its irregular basin are said to be fathomless... and flooded with legends.

One tale ascribed to the lake is that during the 17th century, an Indian Princess was distraught because her father forbid her romance with a white man. The anguished maiden paddled out to the middle of the lake, fastened rocks to her body, and turned herself overboard.

The young woman's body was never recovered from Lake Ronkonkoma, but was found afloat in a Connecticut river. Therefore, the story goes, the Island's Native Americans believed the lake was bottomless and had an underwater connection to Long Island Sound.

The lake has a 70 feet deep "kettle hole" near the northeast shore. Tellers of tales say this is the otherworldly aperture that connects the lake through underwater tunnels to the Sound. Moaning emanates from this corner of the water, whirlpools swirl here, and strange lights appear, all signs that the Lady of the Lake is still consumed with grief.

Another version of the historic yarn is that an Indian princess was betrothed to a young tribesman and the couple was eagerly awaiting their wedding day.

Shortly before they were to wed a white settler slaughtered the innocent brave. The princess was so devastated by the senseless killing of her beloved that she committed suicide by drowning herself in the lake.

As she swam out to the depths, weeping incessantly, she cried out that she would avenge the senseless murder by taking the life, through drowning, of one young male every year. (Suffolk County Police verified one drowning here in 1995.)

Be that as it may, the maiden's ghostly apparition supposedly still walks along Lake Ronkonkoma's shoreline beckoning young men to their watery graves.

Montauk Manor at "The End" of Long Island is a prominent haunted site.

MONTAUK MANOR
Montauk

Supernatural stories swirl about the sprawling Montauk Manor perched high on Signal Hill.

More than any other individual, Carl Fisher made his mark on Montauk. After successfully developing Miami Beach out of a mangrove swamp, the industrialist, who also created the Indianapolis Speedway, turned his sights to the east end of Long Island where he envisioned the "most fabulous summer resort ever imagined in the western world."

In 1926, the multi-millionaire and four partners purchased 9,000 acres on the Montauk peninsula. The centerpiece of his exclusive summer resort was an English Tudor style luxury hotel; the 178-room lodge would be a magnet for the rich and famous.

Work on "Miami Beach of the North" began with forming Montauk Harbor. Fisher dredged a channel between what was then Great Pond and Block Island Sound to create a marina and launch his yacht club.

The fashionable resort sported a beach club, polo fields, golf course, glass enclosed tennis courts, a half-mile boardwalk along the ocean, a ranch, and a health spa. Restaurants served internationally acclaimed cuisine. Croquet players sported on the meticulously manicured lawns. Afternoon tea was sipped on the veranda overlooking the 10,000-acre dreamscape. In short, Montauk Manor was the ultimate in opulence.

Restless souls endure inside Montauk Manor. The most persistent apparition is a Native American who appears in full headdress.

Life was good for Fisher and his lavish undertaking until 1929 when the Great Depression forced his development company into bankruptcy.

The resort revived in 1933 and operated for 30 years as a hotel but again financial difficulties shut its doors.

For over 20 years the brooding behemoth sat empty atop its elevated outlook, a victim of vandalism – a sad, and spooky, landmark indeed.

In 1981, investors rescued the property and by 1985 a $20 million restoration project was complete. Montauk Manor regaled in its original splendor and beauty.

That's when the weirdness began.

As stated in the article "What Haunts Montauk Manor?" by Amanda Star Frazer of *The East Hampton Star*, a female staffer witnessed a figure "bathed in bright light" walk by the door. She described him as tall, with long white hair. There was something unusual about this stranger who stared directly at the captivated worker as he passed by her office. Thinking someone unauthorized was entering the employees' area, she ran to follow the man, but he was nowhere to be found.

Ghostly sightings have occurred on all floors – mostly during the off-season, at dawn, dusk, and during the night.

A female resident claimed that one night her bed lifted five feet off the floor while she was in it, affirmed another employee. (The woman moved to a different floor right after the incident).

A golfer awoke in his room to find a Native American in full headdress standing at the foot of his bed. His two roommates, disturbed from their sleep by his screams, also witnessed the apparition who suddenly departed before their eyes.

Another guest, wrapped in a towel, ran to the lobby and excitedly described a specter peering down at him from a heating vent as he showered. Investigators found nothing amiss.

A local tradesman who worked in the manor one winter snapped pictures of his work. When they were developed one shot revealed a white haze – there was no such fog when he took the picture. Many believe he captured the image of a ghost.

The rambling resort endures adjacent to Fort Hill, site of an ancient Native stronghold. Below lies Massacre Valley where the Montaukett tribe waged war with the Narragansetts in 1654. Montauketts buried their fallen brothers on the Great Hill and their descendents allege that contractors desecrated the "most significant Native American burial ground on the Northeast coast."[vi]

Not only natives died here. In the 1890s, Theodore Roosevelt escorted a regiment of soldiers suffering from yellow fever to the sacred site. Many perished and were temporarily buried on top of the tribal remains.

Perhaps the angry spirits resent the intrusion upon their land and the restless natives rail against the loss of their territory.

40

COUNCIL ROCK

This large white quartz rock was the center of tribal activity for the Montauk Indian Nation. Tribal meetings were held in its shadow and often included representatives of all thirteen tribes that inhabited Long Island.

The Council Rock provided a tangible symbol of the spiritual and political unity of the native peoples of Long Island. Today, it serves as a memorial to the many tribal members buried nearby, and is the historic heart of Montaukett tribal nation.[vii]

Execution Rocks Lighthouse
(U.S. Coast Guard Photo)

EXECUTION ROCKS LIGHTHOUSE
North Hempstead

Execution Rock Lighthouse was built in 1850 to aid mariners sailing around the rocky reefs off Sands Point at the western end of the Long Island Sound. The brown and white lighthouse in Nassau County stands 58 feet tall and shows a white flashing light in the waters approaching New York harbor.

The eerie name spawned from several local 18th century legends.

Folklore says that during the Revolutionary War, British soldiers purportedly abducted American rebels from their settlements and took them to the isolated reef to be tortured and ultimately executed. The Brits chose the secluded spot so as not to provoke further enmity as they chained condemned prisoners to metal spikes driven into the rock, and let them wallow at low tide. When the tide rose, the captives slowly drowned or were ravaged by sharks.

Nautical charts noted the rocky outcropping as "Executioner's Rock" because the rock put to death so many ships. Numerous ships wrecked against the dangerous reef due to insufficient lighting and heavy ship traffic.

Boaters and fishermen claim that the ghosts of the men who died on the reef, whether at the hands of their captors or as victims of shipwrecks, appear near the light station.

Because of the reef's haunted history, supposedly the U. S. Lighthouse Service relieved any keeper from duty who asked – without question. Similarly, any lighthouse keeper assigned to the remote Execution Rocks light station was free to ask for a transfer at any time because service was so lonely that it felt like a "sentence of death."[viii]

RAYNHAM HALL
Oyster Bay

Raynham Hall dates to 1740 when it was center of local affairs in Oyster Bay and home to the prominent Townsend family and members of George Washington's Culper Spy Ring.

During the British occupation of Oyster Bay in 1778, John André, a British major during the Revolutionary War, spent many hours at Raynham Hall visiting with the Townsends who were sharing their home with British Commander Lieutenant Colonel John Simcoe.

One day as André conferred with Simcoe, Sally Townsend overheard them scheming about a payment to Benedict Arnold for the surrender of his troops.

General Benedict Arnold, in reward for his bravery at Saratoga, was placed in charge of West Point, a vital fortification on the Hudson River positioned to protect northern New York from attack. But Arnold, believing that he had not received enough recognition for his services, plotted to turn the fort over to the British.

Through their connections, the Townsends managed to relay the treasonous plot to George Washington and fortunately, for America, Arnold's scheme was thwarted when John André was apprehended at the rendezvous spot. Caught red-handed with Arnold's missive, André was executed and has haunted Raynham Hall ever since. (Arnold fled to England for refuge and died in London in 1801.)

John André is one of Long Island's best-known ghosts. He has haunted this 260-year-old saltbox house at 20 West Main Street in Oyster Bay for over 200 years.

In 1913, Julia Weeks Cole purchased Raynham Hall and was the first to document the ghostly goings on.

Julia wrote in 1938 that she awoke in the middle of the night, looked out the window and spied the ghost of a man on horseback; she suspected it was André.

Docents claim that at least once a year the ghost of a shaggy looking young man, wearing a dark woolen coat with brass buttons and smoking a pipe, walks in the garden. In the house, near the main staircase, a spectral thin man with facial hair, wearing a dark jacket puts in an appearance from time to time. Staffers deduce that these manifestations are Michael Conlin, an Irish immigrant who worked at the home as a servant in the 1860s.

Another Raynham Hall spook is supposed to be Sally Townsend. They say that Sally was in love with John Simcoe, but the commander betrayed her affections. Sally died a spinster at the age of 82 and her unhappy spirit remains in the house. Her bedroom on the second floor is constantly icy cold, even during the summer.

The ghost of a servant woman materialized on at least one occasion in the kitchen. She could be the spirit responsible for the delicious scent of baking apples quite commonly experienced.

Electronic voice phenomenon (EVP) is the recording of intelligible voices on tape that has no known physical explanation. Long Island ghost investigators captured spine-tingling voices saying, "Yes, there is," "Be patient," "Yes... I am," "I'm mad at you," "Shhhhhh," and "I want outta here" in response to the researchers' questions.

Other traces of paranormal phenomena include the smell of whiskey at times, and a rosy aroma wafting through the historic, and *very* haunted, home.

WOODWARD ESTATE
Oyster Bay

On October 30, 1955, Ann Woodward shot her husband, William, twice in the neck virtually decapitating him. A grand jury believed her story that she had mistaken "Billy" for a prowler who had recently broken into neighboring houses.

Conversely, New York society mavens believed she deliberately murdered her husband in their Oyster Bay home and that her formidable mother-in-law, Elsie Woodward, covered up the crime to prevent further scandal to the socially prominent family.

For decades controversy swirled over whether Ann intentionally gunned down her husband.

Truman Capote fictionalized the incident in a malicious 1975 *Esquire* story, which drove Ann to suicide, and later Dominick Dunne was inspired by the event to pen *The Two Mrs. Grenvilles*.

For years locals buzzed that Billy's headless form still roamed his mortal home. Monica Randall, ghost hunter and author of *The Mansions of Long Island's Gold Coast*, believes the Woodward estate is genuinely haunted.

According to *Newsday*,[ix] Randall, Dunne, and a psychic, performed a séance on All Hallows Eve in 1982. The trio was situated close by the spot where the actual killing took place when a World War II medal materialized out of thin air. Randall later verified that Woodward was indeed the recipient of the award.

EPISCOPAL CEMETERY
Patchogue

As early as the late 1800s, the *Brooklyn Eagle* newspaper chronicled Long Island's ghosts. An article in the February 28, 1895 edition reported on an ethereal form that haunted the "Lake View Cemetery," also called the "Episcopal Cemetery," situated on Blood Hill and adjoining the property of the Patchogue - Plymouth lace factory.

The ghostly meanderings terrorized the young female workers on their way home and townsfolk refused to go out after dark.

Every night at sundown the phenomena started with an ungodly moan emanating from the cemetery. Then a headless figure would slowly rise from the grave of three sailors, victims of the ill-fated schooner *Louis V. Place* that had earlier been wrecked off the coast.

The apparition gradually levitated from the ground and floated toward a tree planted upon the site previously occupied by a reputed haunted house. Once the entity settled down, it began to flail its arms.

Renowned author and poet, Madame Oakes-Smith, was an eccentric who shared the property with her equally odd husband until 1867. The home lay vacant and gained a ghostly reputation, no doubt due to its previous tenants; the structure eventually burned to the ground.

Villagers speculated the silly specter was Mr. Smith.

HOUSE on CARLTON STREET
Port Washington

During the 1960s, a private home on Carlton Street was plagued by the phantom of a tall young man. The disconcerting sightings of his specter were limited to the second floor in the 85 year old home. A thirteen-year-old girl who lived in the house said she often saw the ghost pacing the hallway throughout the night.

The ghostly boy's inopportune appearances knew no boundaries; he would open the bathroom door while the residents were bathing or sneak into the bedroom during intimate moments.

Many residents heard the inexplicable creaking of the second story floorboards and the door to the second floor bathroom would always open of its own accord no matter how tightly shut.

The spirit went to extremes when he pushed a woman down the flight of stairs disabling her for several months.

BYRAM HOUSE
Sag Harbor

The black Italianate villa that overlooks Oakland Cemetery was home to astronomer and clockmaker Ephraim Byram. Built by his father in 1852, Ephraim and his wife, who was a spiritualist, lived in the quaint cottage topped with a square tower that Byram used as an observatory.

Every evening and into the wee hours of the morning, Byram peered at the night sky through his telescope. The stargazer stood six feet, six inches tall and was quite a sight as he roamed the village streets in his two-foot-high stovepipe hat.

The eccentric scientist designed steeple clocks for the Sag Harbor Methodist Church, the Old Whalers Church, and City Hall in lower Manhattan.

After Byram's death in 1881, his wife, who practiced homeopathic medicine, often conducted séances in the house, inciting rumors that the house was haunted. Children, and locals alike, crossed the street to avoid passing by the eerie house.

HISTORIC HOMES
Sag Harbor

When the English arrived on Long Island's South Fork in the mid-17th century, they discovered deep water on the bay side, a convenient port to moor ocean-going vessels burgeoning with cargo. The location was also handy for ocean side, Sagaponack farmers who could easily ride their carts there to meet the incoming boats.

Overtime, the large meadow facing the wharf took on the name Sagaponack Harbor. Eventually it was shortened to Sag Harbor and by the mid-18th century, houses appeared on the horizon.

Sag Harbor quickly evolved into a great whaling community and became a trend-setting village. The town boasted the first seaport in the region and was home to the first U. S. Customs House on Long Island. Sag Harbor introduced the Island's first newspaper and launched the practice of milk delivery to front doors.

The bustling village teemed with people from all over the world. Harboring ships held crews of American Indians, Polynesians, runaway slaves from the South, Africans and aborigines from Australia.[x]

At the time Sag Harbor was like no other place in America. In an 1843 history of New York, the author claimed that there were only two places of any significance in the state, Brooklyn on the Island's West End and Sag Harbor on the East End.

Given such a background, it's no wonder that spirits still make their home in the historic town.

Richard Barons, Director of the Southampton Historical Museum, is a collector of true ghost stories, and he shares his spooky tales with the public at various Long Island venues.

One favorite is a story about a house with eyebrow windows in Sag Harbor's historic district.

Back in the 1950s, the owner left the house to run errands. When she got into her car, she noticed a faint light in the attic. For years, no one had ventured into the garret, and come to think of it, there's no electricity up there.

Concerned about a sparking wire in the 1860s house, the woman goes back in and trudges up the stairs with a flashlight. Finding nothing amiss, she locks up the house, goes outside and, luckily, sees no glow in the decorative window.

A week later a neighbor mentions that he noticed a light left on in the woman's attic night after night. Totally baffled, the owner goes upstairs again and carefully checks the eaves. At last, she discovers a 19th century oil lamp sitting on a crate facing the window over the front door. She takes the light downstairs to the living room.

One night, she awakens and hears a noise, like a branch hitting the window. Unable to sleep, she trundles downstairs, peers into the parlor, and lo and behold, the lamp is lit!

Totally perplexed, she rationalizes that the lamp isn't lit at all - the glow is just a reflection off its pewter surface. Nevertheless, to allay her nagging misgivings, she puts the lamp in a closet and forgets about it.

Several years later the woman rents out the house and goes to Europe.

During her stay overseas, she receives correspondence from the tenant. He wonders about a light coming from under the closet door. At once she knows exactly what the light source is but the door is locked and the renter can't do anything about it.

Immediately, upon her arrival home she sells the lamp to a local antique dealer.

What could have caused the ghostly glow? Did the woman's house harbor a spirit from the past? We will never know, that is unless someone else comes forward with a story about this strange lantern...

Sag Harbor's ghost connoisseur tells another true tale about a historic home on the town's Main Street.

Visitors report that during the night, they hear a noise in the hallway that wakes them. The guest then realizes that the bedroom is freezing cold and gets a whiff of exotic incense, like the kind used in church. The occupant's gaze falls upon the closed bedroom door – it's oddly transparent, they can see right through it... Standing in the doorway is an old woman dressed in a flannel nightgown and cap. The gaunt ghoul stands perfectly still and stares into the room. Moments later, the room warms up, the scent dissipates, and the ghost dissolves.

This haunting has occurred since the 1930s, and to this day unnerved guests arrive at the breakfast table eager to share their chilling tale over a cup of hot coffee.

HERRMANN HOUSE
Seaford

At 3:30 P. M., on February 3, 1958, a Long Island family witnessed bottles of bleach, liquid starch, medicine, nail polish, shampoo, and even holy water pop their caps and topple over. Thus began one of the most notorious, and documented, poltergeist hauntings in history.

Air France employee James Herrmann, his wife, and their two children observed bottles spin off their lids, turn on the shelves, and fall to the floor. Herrmann watched a prescription bottle hop at least six inches across a bathroom vanity into the sink.

The Herrmanns named their poltergeist "Popper."

At first, the paranormal performance was slow – only one or two manifestations a day. After a few weeks, the supernatural events intensified and became violent.

Once a bottle of ink flew from the dining table and slammed against the front door, spattering the portal and everything surrounding it. A sugar bowl suddenly lifted off the kitchen table and crashed onto the floor.

Many witnessed the supernatural episodes. A British photographer saw one of his flashbulbs levitate from an end table.

On two occasions a Nassau County detective heard noises in adjoining rooms. When he ran into the dinette to investigate, he found that a bowl had flipped three feet. In the son's bedroom, a chest of drawers tipped over and the boy's phonograph was spinning around the room!

A *Newsday* reporter said he heard a crash from the living room and discovered that the mischievous spirit had smashed a porcelain statuette against the wooden desk, denting it. Then a cardboard globe silently spun out of control and hurtled down a hallway narrowly missing a police officer who was probing the place for possible explanations.

The Air Force thought vibrations from overhead jets were to blame, but a vibration detector set up by Long Island Lighting Company found nothing amiss. RCA technicians detected no abnormal signals. The Town of Hempstead Building Department discerned no defects in the Herrmann's 5-year-old house.

Duke University had its premier parapsychologists investigate. They produced a 45-page study delineating the unexplainable phenomena (on file at the university).

Originally the thought was the manifestations were caused by psychokinetic energy from the teenagers, often poltergeist activity centers on children, especially during puberty, but the odd goings-on occurred when the Herrmann offspring weren't even around so that theory was ruled out.

Night tables turned over, bookcases upended, and by last count, 67 uncanny incidents occurred inside the troubled house before the bizarre events suddenly ceased on March 2nd.

BABY GHOST
Southampton

Since ghostly tales involve people who were once alive, the stories are actually sadder then they are scary. Historian Richard Barons offers a poignant tale that occurred in a home off Southampton's Gin Lane.

A couple bought the 19th century dwelling, which featured a beautiful curved staircase, as a summer place. Eventually they visited on weekends in the off-season.

Relaxing in the living room one evening, they heard a strange sound like something bouncing down steps. They look, but find nothing. For two years they've owned the house and have only stayed there in the peak season when the house teemed with people. This time it's different; the house is quiet with just the two of them.

A few nights later, the same bouncing sound on the stairs awakens the husband and leaves him puzzled.

Days go by and while attending a local gathering a guest inquires, "What house do you live in?" Like many Southampton houses it's known by the name of the family who built it, so the man replies with the name. The guest counters with, "Oh, that's such a tragic house."

It turns out that a few years after the house opened, the owners threw an extravagant party. Even though the couples' three year old was attended by a nanny, he alluded her supervision, crawled out of bed and fell to his death while chasing his errant ball that had rolled down the beautiful staircase.

*The picturesque Wind Hill Windmill carries on as the symbol of
Southampton College and harbors a petite presence -
a sad and lonely reminder of its tragic past.*

HAUNTED WINDMILL
Southampton

Eastern Long Island boasts the largest collection of surviving windmills in the United States. Looked upon as picturesque and quaint relics of the past, windmills actually functioned as vital labor saving devices for early settlers. They facilitated the grinding of corn and grain, the pumping of water, the sawing of wood, and various other essential chores.

The Southampton College Windmill, situated on a campus knoll that overlooks Shinnecock Hills, is known historically as the Mill Hill Windmill and originally stood in Southampton Village.

Constructed in 1712, the three-story, gray-shingled structure served as a landmark for seafarers until Mrs. William S. Hoyt, the daughter of Abraham Lincoln's Secretary of the Navy, Salmon P. Chase, purchased the windmill in 1890 and moved the artifact to her property for use as a tearoom and playhouse.

Six years later, wealthy textile manufacturer, Arthur B. Claflin, bought the Hoyt estate and the picturesque windmill became a guest cottage, and home to playwright Tennessee Williams for a while.

But there seems to be one occupant that lingers inside the weathered space – the spirit of a little girl.

Claflin's daughter loved to frolic in the distinctive structure. The word is that her play turned tragic when she fell down the steep stairs and died from her injuries.

As maintained by untold students, the young girl's ghost inhabits her playhouse; her innocent face often peers from the pint-sized windows. Captivated students say they "feel" her presence and assert that the windmill generates a supernatural "vibe."

Electro-magnetic field (EMF) detection meters are used to seek out disruptions in the natural magnetic field of the environment. They help to authenticate evidence of paranormal activity. Ghost hunters' meters register an unusually high magnetic field on the windmill's rise.

Undergrads sense someone staring at them as they pass the place at night and insist a tiny, indistinct voice calls out to them. Sensitive students get the impression that the spirit of Claflin's lonely daughter is looking for a playmate.

The girl's apparition appears in every window; because of her diminutive size, only her head and shoulders are visible. Her tiny face follows passersby and is seen gazing out from window to window.

The historic and picturesque windmill carries on as the symbol of Southampton College signifying the history and traditions of eastern Long Island – its petite presence a sad and lonely reminder of its tragic past.

PEACE AND PLENTY INN
South Huntington

Now a private residence, the Peace and Plenty Inn was the center of West Hills civic and social life before, during, and after the Revolutionary War.

Walt Whitman, who lived nearby, frequented the tavern and President Theodore Roosevelt and members of his family often visited the Peace and Plenty Inn, usually on horseback, attracting the public's attention and prompting development in the area.

Built in 1680, the inn remained in the Chichester family for several generations until the 20th century.

Kerriann Brosky tells the history of the ancient house in *Huntington's Hidden Past.*

James and Mary Chichester moved from Salem, Massachusetts to Huntington in 1653 and opened an inn.

The innkeeper was an important citizen back in the 17th century. Known as an "ordinary," the inn served as a central gathering place for the community as well as travelers, and was strictly supervised by town officials. There were no computers, radios, or televisions; people exchanged news and were entertained at the ordinary.

Asa Chichester was the last of his clan to run the inn. When the Jericho Turnpike was extended into Huntington in the late 1800s, business declined at the Peace and Plenty. Asa had no choice but to turn the place into a boarding house.

Many believe ghosts haunt the historic edifice on Chichester Road.

At one time, lamps and candles disappeared without a trace. Was Asa the culprit gathering lights to keep the tavern lit? Disembodied footsteps echoed as an unseen specter walked through the space opening doors as he performed his otherworldly duties.

Chichester family members are buried nearby. Do their spirits visit their mortal digs during the night to ponder the modern communication devices? What else can explain the television turning on and changing channels when no one is in the room? Why does the radio suddenly blare during the night?

Who, or what, keeps the family's dog at bay, stubbornly refusing to enter the most ancient rooms?

In a building that has witnessed over 300 years of history, it's anyone's guess.

The Peace and Plenty Inn houses spirits of the Chichester clan.
(Photo source: www.lieye.com)

ALICE PARSONS' HOME
Stony Brook

Suffolk County's oldest murder case remains unresolved.

On June 9, 1937, Alice Parsons disappeared from her squab farm in Stony Brook. The niece of Brooklyn-Manhattan Transit Company founder Timothy Shaler Williams, Alice was 38 when she went missing.

News reports described her as a woman who lived a life in contrast to her blue-blood heritage by dressing sensibly and raising squabs on a modest 11-acre farm she owned with her husband, Will.

Will was the son of a wealthy paper manufacturer, a Yale graduate, a U. S. Navy veteran of World War I, and a social climber.

On the day she went missing, Alice purportedly drove her husband to the railroad station. That was the last time she was ever seen alive.

Some told police that an unknown couple drove up to the Parsons house and that Alice left with them, supposedly to show them around her family's estate that was on the market.

On June 10th, a ransom note was found in Parsons' car, which was parked in their garage.

The Federal Bureau of Investigation joined in the search – even then FBI Director J. Edgar Hoover visited the farm. The agency withdrew from the case a year later.

Will Parsons and their housekeeper, "Countess" Anna Kupryanova, who allegedly fled Russia after the Communist revolution, were the chief suspects. The pair soon moved to Carmel, California and was married in 1940.

Six years later, Alice Parsons was declared legally dead, and her brother and husband were in dispute over her two wills. Even though both bequeathed most of her estate to her husband and Kupryanova, the couple settled by renouncing their claim.

Before Alice Parsons' home inexplicably burned to the ground in 1997, realtors alleged the house was haunted. Doors opened and closed spontaneously and out of the blue rocking chairs rocked. The basement exuded an eerie atmosphere.

When writer Rosalie Niemczyk was researching her book, *Second Harvest: The Alice Parsons Story*, she visited the house and called out to Alice while in the creepy cellar. All of a sudden an ice-cold draft swept over the author.

The house went up in flames shortly thereafter.

COUNTRY HOUSE RESTAURANT
Stony Brook

Annette Williamson sided with the British during the Revolutionary War and her allegiance cost Williamson her life. She was hanged as a spy by loyalist troops and buried next to her kin in a small cemetery somewhere on the property now occupied by the Country House Restaurant.

The woman's spirit has taken refuge inside the eatery and usually makes its presence known in the kitchen. Stunningly, her full-bodied apparition also appears on the staircase.

Once a towel floated by several witnesses and a news reporter had a glass of wine thrown in his face by the perturbed spirit.

The building on Route 25A was originally constructed in 1710 by Obadiah Davis as a farmhouse. Eventually the structure became an inn and stagecoach stop. In 1838, Thomas Hadaway, an English actor and comedian, bought the house and named it the Hadaway House Restaurant.

Hadaway conducted many séances at the inn. One in attendance was his neighbor, Long Island artist William Sidney Mount.[1] Allegedly Rembrandt was contacted through the séances and Mount felt that the 17th century painter helped him with his craft.

---

[1] See page 69.

*The Country House Restaurant is home to
a Revolutionary ghost.*

Annette Williamson was executed by the British during the Revolutionary War and is buried in a small cemetery on the property now occupied by the Country House Restaurant.

The present day rustic restaurant opened in 1967 and has been a reputed haunted spot for many years.

Parapsychologists have investigated the spooky allegations and purportedly contacted the spirit of a young woman who claimed that she and her family lived in the old house. She said she was the last of them to die – lynched for her disloyalty during the War for Independence.

The unexplainable events that occur here are strange but not scary. Staffers will shut off all the lights before they leave, but by the time they're out in the parking lot, the place is ablaze with light.

Sometimes it's impossible to enter the upstairs room where supposedly Annette resided – the door just won't budge.

Those who work at the restaurant feel the spirit of the revolutionary entity still resides in the house going about her day-to-day activities. Her presence is friendly and they feel comfortable having her around.

HAWKINS-MOUNT HOUSE
Stony Brook

At the corner of Route 25A and Stony Brook Road stands the rambling Hawkins-Mount House. Operated by the Museums at Stony Brook, the house is not open to the public.

The original section of the house went up in 1725 and gradually increased in size with each addition tacked on by two subsequent residents – first Eleazer Hawkins in 1757 and then Jonas Hawkins who transformed the property into a store and tavern in the late 1700s. "Jonas Hawkins Store and Ordinary" was two and one half stories and contained twenty rooms.

During the Revolutionary War, Jonas Hawkins operated as a messenger for George Washington as a member of the Culper Spy Ring.

In the 1800s the family of artist William Sidney Mount lived in the house. Mount was a painter from Stony Brook who achieved fame in Europe as well as America. The house still retains the work of art on the attic ceiling that William painted.

William Sidney Mount (1807-1868) is widely credited for the creation of American Genre Painting. His realistic scenery and everyday subject matter made him popular with the public and critics, and he was highly regarded as one of the great American talents of his time.

A Long Island native from Setauket, Mount began his career at seventeen as a sign painter. He soon advanced

*The spirit of artist William Sidney Mount's cousin
used to frequent the Hawkins-Mount House.*

beyond advertisements to the National Academy of Design as a student of history painting, which inspired him to paint portraits and genre scenes.

Surprisingly, it is Elizabeth Mount, the artist's first cousin, who haunts the landmark, yellow house.

Shortly after William died in 1868, rumors began to spread that the house was haunted.

In 1960, a 5-year-old girl, living in the house and also named Elizabeth, said she saw a lady in a white gown standing at the foot of her bed. The lady welcomed the child to the house and told her that she would be very happy there.

After that faucets began to mysteriously turn on. One time, little Elizabeth's mother was splashed with water in a section of the house that had no water source.

Although there have been no more reports of unearthly happenings, possibly Elizabeth wanted to emulate her cousin and be an artist, and the reason her spirit called out from beyond the grave was to announce her desire to paint with *water* colors.

PRIVATE RESIDENCE
Wantagh

This is a story about four men who live in Wantagh in a haunted house. Their place is possessed by a soldier's spirit and although they do not know his name, rank or serial number, they do know that the flag that draped his coffin lies on a shelf in a closet. The colors remain untouched and undisturbed and will continue to do so indefinitely...

The man who resided in the house before them was a veteran of World War II. When he died, his wife sold the house and left behind all her husband's personal belongings including the flag that covered his coffin. The new owners tried to return the items to the family but they were never claimed.

Two brothers have lived in the house for over twenty years and during that time experienced lights, television, and other electronics turning on and off "all the time," spongy Frisbees flying across the room, and the sound of footsteps walking up and down the stairs. (As is the case in many hauntings, the paranormal activity centers on the staircase). "Something" moves in the closet and a clock without batteries chimes every hour.

One night as one of the brothers lay in his bed a terrifying bolt of lightening blew the power out. As a thunderstorm raged, apparitions of only a face and wringing hands formed in the chair and the chilling materialization whispered his name.

ACKNOWLEDGEMENTS

I want to thank my childhood friend, Bridget McMahon Carles, for her loyal camaraderie and for accompanying me on a magical jaunt to Long Island. Friends since kindergarten, Bridget and I have shared many spirited occasions including a trip to Big Moose Lake where Grace Brown's ghost appeared to us. That event prompted me to chronicle true ghost stories, and thus, live my dream.

Bridget McMahon Carles

BIBLIOGRAPHY

"A Spellbinder Right Out of Hollywood Lingers on Island 60 Years Later." *Newsday*, December 1, 1995.

Bellows, Charles. "Return the Windmill." *Dan's Papers*, September 3, 2004.

Bernstein, Jim and Bratskeir, Anne. "Vital Signs, Taking the Pulse of Life on Long Island." *Newsday*, October 27, 1996.

Brosky, Kerriann Flanagan. *Huntington's Hidden Past*. Maple Hill Press, Huntington, NY; 1995.

Chester, Marjorie. "Design: An Italianate Villa." *The East Hampton Star*, January 3, 2002.

Fox, Tristram. "Unknown Soldier." *Paranormal P.I.*, Long Island Press: www.longislandpress.com.

Frazer, Amanda Star. "What Haunts Montauk Manor?" *The East Hampton Star*, October 25, 2001.

Hauck, Dennis William. *The National Directory of Haunted Places*. Penguin Books, New York, NY; 1996.

Hinkle, Annette. "Chilling Nighttime Tales." *The Sag Harbor Express*, October 24, 2002.

_____. "Terrifyingly True Tales, And Other Bumps in the Night." *The Sag Harbor Express*, October 30, 2003.

Merritt, Jim. "Stalking Specters." *Newsday*: October 29, 2000.

Morris, Thomas. "Brentwood, A Place Built on Dreams." (www.newsday.com).

Randall, Monica. *Winfield*. St. Martin's Press, New York, NY; 2003.

Scroope, Kristin E. "The Legends of Execution Rock." (www.scroope.net/longislandlighthouses).

Smitten, Susan. *Ghost Stories of New York State*. Long Pine Publishing, Auburn, WA; 2004.

Steiger, Brad. *Real Ghosts, Restless Spirits, and Haunted Places*. Visible Ink Press, Canton, MI; 2003.

Twarowski, Christopher. "Long Island's Haunted Halloween Guide." The New Island Ear: www.islandear.com.

Wax, Emily. "Visiting the Local Haunts." *Newsday*: October 26, 1997.

Wick, Steve. "Sag Harbor's Heyday." (www.newsday.com).

Zezima, Jerry. "In Spirited Company." *Newsday*: October 25, 1998.

WEBSITES

Getting Curious about the Past: www.lihistory.com
Long Island Lighthouse Society: www.longislandlighthouses.com
Long Island Ghost Hunters: wwwlongislandghosthunters.com
Long Island Paranormal Hunters: www.paranormal-hunters.com
Newsday: www.newsday.com
Raynham Hall Museum: www.raynhamhallmuseum.org
Sagtikos Historic Society: www.sagtikosmanor.com

ENDNOTES

[i] Thomas Morris, "Brentwood, A Place Built on Dreams," (newsday.com).
[ii] Dennis William Hauck, *National Directory of Haunted Places*, .
[iii] Monica Randall, *Winfield*, 119.
[iv] Randall, 218.
[v] Kerriann Flanagan Brosky, *Huntington's Hidden Past*, 130-133.
[vi] Amanda Star Frazer, "What Haunts Montauk Manor?" (*The East Hampton Star*).
[vii] Taken from the commemorative plaque in Fort Hill Cemetery, Montauk.
[viii] Kristin E. Scroope, "The Legends of Execution Rock," (www.scroope.net).
[ix] Jim Merritt, "Stalking Specters," (*Newsday*).
[x] Steve Wick, "Sag Harbor's Heyday," (newsday.com).

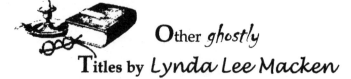

Other *ghostly*
Titles by *Lynda Lee Macken*

ADIRONDACK GHOSTS ~ Volumes I & II

EMPIRE GHOSTS
New York State's Haunted Landmarks

GHOSTLY GOTHAM
New York City's Haunted History

HAUNTED HISTORY OF STATEN ISLAND

GHOSTS OF THE GARDEN STATE
Volumes I & II

HAUNTED CAPE MAY

HAUNTED SALEM & BEYOND

HAUNTED BALTIMORE

BLACK CAT PRESS
Post Office Box 1218, Forked River, New Jersey 08731

E-mail: llmacken@hotmail.com